My Shadow
and other poems

Compiled by Tig Thomas

Miles Kelly

My Treasures

These nuts, that I keep in the back of the nest,
Where all my tin soldiers are lying at rest,
Were gathered in Autumn by nursie and me
In a wood with a well by the side of the sea.

This whistle we made and how clearly it sounds!
By the side of a field at the end of the grounds.
Of a branch of a plane, with a knife of
    my own,
It was nursie who made it,
    and nursie alone!

The stone, with the white and the yellow and grey,
We discovered I cannot tell HOW far away;
And I carried it back although weary and cold,
For though father denies it, I'm sure it is gold.

But of all my treasures the last is the king,
For there's very few children possess such a thing;
And that is a chisel, both handle and blade,
Which a man who was really a
carpenter made.

Robert Louis Stevenson

My Books

I love my books
They are the homes
of queens and fairies,
Knights and gnomes.

Each time I read I make a call
On some quaint person large or small,
Who welcomes me with hearty hand
And leads me through his wonderland.

Each book is like
A city street
Along whose winding way I meet
New friends and old who laugh and sing
And take me off adventuring!

Anonymous

Extremes

A little boy once played so loud
That the Thunder, up in a thunder-cloud,
Said,

**"Since I can't be heard, why, then,
I'll never, never thunder again!"**

And a little girl once kept so still
That she heard a fly on the window-sill
Whisper and say to a lady-bird,

**"She is the stilliest child I
ever heard!"**

James Whitcomb Riley

The Worm

No, little worm, you need not slip
Into your hole, with such a skip;
Drawing the gravel as you glide
On to your smooth and slimy side.
I'm not a crow, poor worm, not I,
Peeping about your holes to spy,
And fly away with you in air,
To give my young ones each a share.

No, and I'm not a rolling-stone,
Creaking along with hollow groan;
Nor am I of the naughty crew,
Who don't care what poor worms go through,
But trample on them as they lie,
Rather than pass them gently by;
Or keep them dangling on a hook,
Choked in a dismal pond or brook,
Till some poor fish comes swimming past,
And finishes their pain at last.

For my part, I could never bear
 Your tender flesh to hack and tear,
   Forgetting that poor worms endure
    As much as I should, to be sure,
     If any giant should come and jump
     On to my back, and kill me plump,
      Or run my heart through with a scythe,
     And think it fun to see me writhe!
O no, I'm only looking about,
To see you wriggle in and out,
And drawing together your slimy rings,
Instead of feet, like other things:
So, little worm, don't slide and slip
Into your hole, with such a skip.

Ann Taylor

Peek-a-Boo

The cunningest thing that a baby can do
Is the very first time it plays peek-a-boo;

When it hides its pink little face in its hands,
And crows, and shows that it understands

What nurse, and mamma and papa, too,
Mean when they hide and cry,

"peek-a-boo, peek-a-boo."

Oh, what a wonderful thing it is,
When they find that baby can play like this;

And everyone listens, and thinks it true
That baby's gurgle means

"peek-a-boo, peek-a-boo."

And over and over the changes are rung
On the marvellous infant who talks so young.

I wonder if anyone ever knew
A baby that never played
"peek-a-boo, peek-a-boo."

'Tis old as the hills are. I believe
Cain was taught it by Mother Eve;

For Cain was an innocent baby, too,
And I am sure he played

"peek-a-boo, peek-a-boo."

And the whole world full of the children of men,
Have all of them played that game since then.

Kings and princes and beggars, too,
Everyone has played

"peek-a-boo, peek-a-boo."

Thief and robber and ruffian bold,
The crazy tramp and the drunkard old,

All have been babies who laughed and knew
How to hide, and play

"peek-a-boo, peek-a-boo."

Ella Wheeler Wilcox

Riddle: Thomas a Tattamus

Thomas a Tattamus took two Ts,
To tie two tups to two tall trees,
To frighten the terrible Thomas a Tattamus!
Tell me how many Ts there are in all **THAT**.

Answer: Two — the question asked how many Ts there were in 'that'.

13

My Kingdom

Down by a shining water well
I found a very little dell,
No higher than my head.
The heather and the gorse about
In summer bloom were coming out,
Some yellow and some red.

I called the little pool a sea;
The little hills were big to me;
For I am very small.
I made a boat, I made a town,
I searched the caverns up and down,
And named them one and all.

And all about was mine, I said,
The little sparrows overhead,
The little minnows too.
This was the world and I was king;
For me the bees came by to sing,
For me the swallows flew.

I played there were no deeper seas,
Nor any wider plains than these,
Nor other kings than me.
At last I heard my mother call
Out from the house at evenfall,
To call me home to tea.

And I must rise and leave my dell,
And leave my dimpled water well,
And leave my heather blooms.
Alas! And as my home I neared,
How very big my nurse appeared.
How great and cool the rooms!

Robert Louis Stevenson

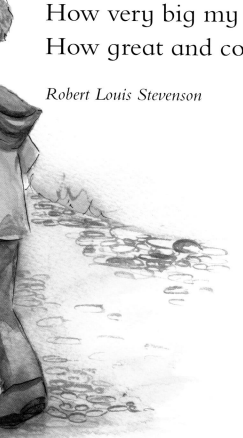

From *Night*

The sun descending in the west,
The evening star does shine;
The birds are silent in their nest,
And I must seek for mine.
The moon like a flower,
In heaven's high bower,
With silent delight
Sits and smiles on the night.

William Blake

Betty Botter Bought some Butter

Betty Botter bought some butter,
But, she said, this butter's bitter;
If I put it in my batter
It will make my batter bitter.
But a bit of better butter
Will make my batter better.

So she bought a bit of butter
Better than her bitter butter,
And she put it in her batter
And the batter was not bitter.
So, 'twas better Betty Botter
Bought a bit of better butter.

Anonymous

Little Tommy Tucker

Little Tommy Tucker
Sings for his supper;
What shall we give him
Brown bread and butter.
How shall he cut it
Without any knife?
How shall he marry
Without any wife?

Anonymous

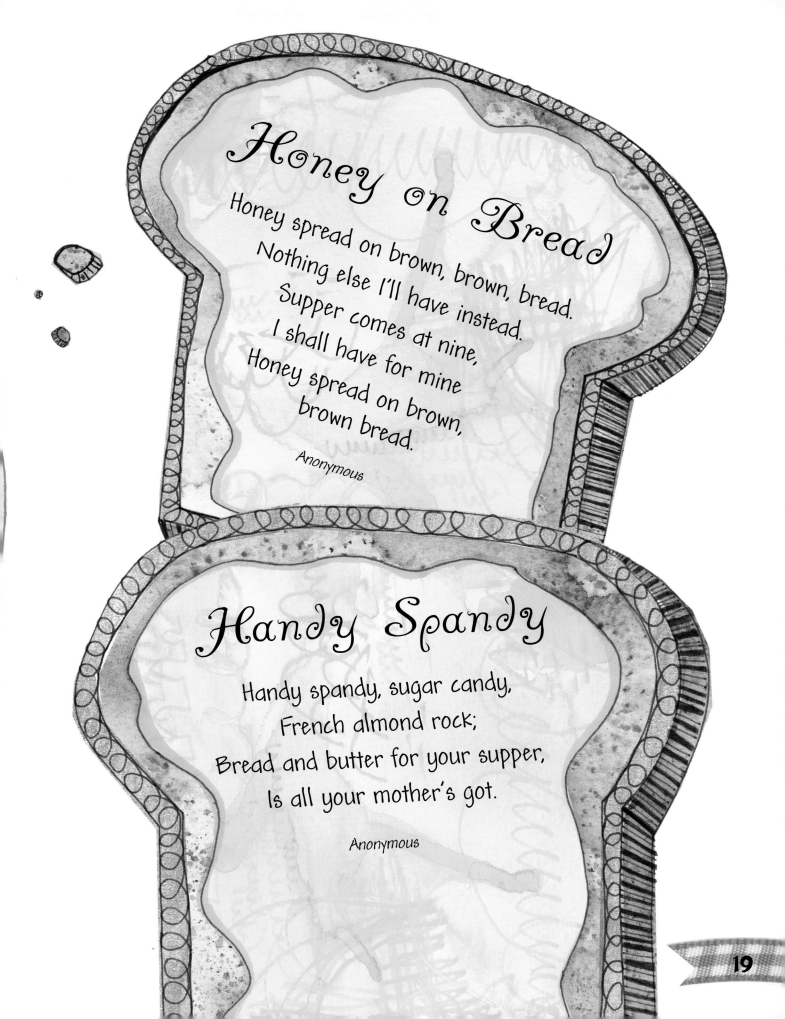

Honey on Bread

Honey spread on brown, brown, bread.
Nothing else I'll have instead.
Supper comes at nine,
I shall have for mine
Honey spread on brown,
brown bread.

Anonymous

Handy Spandy

Handy spandy, sugar candy,
French almond rock;
Bread and butter for your supper,
Is all your mother's got.

Anonymous

This poem is sung by the mock turtle in Lewis Carroll's Alice in Wonderland.

Beautiful Soup

Beautiful Soup, so rich and green,
Waiting in a hot tureen!
Who for such dainties would not stoop?
Soup of the evening, beautiful Soup!
Soup of the evening, beautiful Soup!
Beau-ootiful Soo-oop!
Beau-ootiful Soo-oop!
Soo-oop of the e-e-evening,
Beautiful, beautiful Soup!

Beautiful Soup! Who cares for fish,
Game, or any other dish?
Who would not give all else for two
Pennyworth only of Beautiful Soup?
Pennyworth only of beautiful Soup?
Beau-ootiful Soo-oop!
Beau-ootiful Soo-oop!
Soo-oop of the e-e-evening,
Beautiful, beauti-ful soup!

Lewis Carroll

Wash the Dishes

Wash the dishes,
Wipe the dishes,
Ring the bell for tea.

Three good wishes,
Three good kisses,
I will give to thee.

Anonymous

Coffee and Tea

Molly my sister and I fell out,
And what do you think it was all about?
She loved coffee and I loved tea,
And that was the reason we couldn't agree!

Anonymous

Bessie's Song to her Doll

Matilda Jane, you never look
At any toy or picture-book.
I show you pretty things in vain —
You must be blind, Matilda Jane!

I ask you riddles, tell you tales,
But all our conversation fails.
You never answer me again —
I fear you're dumb, Matilda Jane!

Matilda darling, when I call,
You never seem to hear at all.
I shout with all my might and main —
But you're so deaf, Matilda Jane!

Matilda Jane, you needn't mind,
For, though you're deaf and dumb and blind,
There's some one loves you, it is plain —
And that is me, Matilda Jane!

Lewis Carroll

Our Mother

Hundreds of stars in the pretty sky,
Hundreds of shells on the shore together,
Hundreds of birds that go singing by,
Hundreds of birds in the sunny weather,
Hundreds of dewdrops to greet
   the dawn,
Hundreds of bees in the
   purple clover,
Hundreds of butterflies on
   the lawn,
But only one mother the
   wide world over.

George Cooper

23

This is a counting game to play with cherry or plum stones – the answer tells you your fortune in love.

One I Love

One I love;
Two, I love;
Three, I love, I say;
Four, I love with all my heart;
Five, I cast away;
Six, he loves,
Seven, she loves;
Eight, both love;
Nine, he comes;
Ten, he tarries;
Eleven, he courts; and
Twelve, he marries.

Anonymous

Tarries delays or waits too long

24

He Loves Me

He loves me
He don't
He'll marry me
He won't
He would if he
could but he can't.

Anonymous

The Lost Doll

I once had a sweet little doll, dears,
The prettiest doll in the world;
Her cheeks were so red and white, dears,
And her hair was so charmingly curled.
But I lost my poor little doll, dears,
As I played on the heath one day;
And I cried for her more than a week, dears,
But I never could find where she lay.

I found my poor little doll, dears,
As I played on the heath one day;
Folks say she is terribly changed, dears,
For her paint is all washed away,
And her arms trodden off by the cows, dears,
And her hair not the least bit curled;
Yet for old sake's sake, she is still, dears,
The prettiest doll in the world.

Charles Kingsley

The Unseen Playmate

When children are playing alone on the green,
In comes the playmate that never was seen.
When children are happy and lonely and good,
The Friend of the Children comes out of the wood.

Nobody heard him, and nobody saw,
His is a picture you never could draw,
But he's sure to be present, abroad or at home,
When children are happy and playing alone.

He lies in the laurels, he runs on the grass,
He sings when you tinkle the musical glass;
Whene'er you are happy and cannot tell why,
The Friend of the Children is sure to be by!

He loves to be little, he hates to be big,
'Tis he that inhabits the caves that you dig;
'Tis he when you play with your soldiers of tin
That sides with the Frenchmen and never can win.

'Tis he, when at night you go off to your bed,
Bids you go to sleep and not trouble your head;
For wherever they're lying, in cupboard or shelf,
'Tis he will take care of your playthings himself!

Robert Louis Stevenson

A Good Play

We built a ship upon the stairs
All made of the back-bedroom chairs,
And filled it full of sofa pillows
To go a-sailing on the billows.

We took a saw and several nails,
And water in the nursery pails;
And Tom said, "Let us also take
An apple and a slice of cake;"
Which was enough for Tom and me
To go a-sailing on, till tea.

We sailed along for days
    and days,
And had the very best
    of plays;
But Tom fell out and
    hurt his knee,
So there was no one left
    but me.

Robert Louis Stevenson

At the Seaside

When I was down beside the sea
A wooden spade they gave to me
To dig the sandy shore.
My holes were empty like a cup.
In every hole the sea came up,
Till it could come no more.

Robert Louis Stevenson

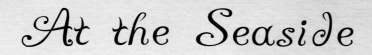

The Children's Hour

Between the dark and the daylight,
    When the night is beginning to lower,
Comes a pause in the day's occupations,
    That is known as the Children's Hour.

I hear in the chamber above me
    The patter of little feet,
The sound of a door that is opened,
    And voices soft and sweet.

From my study I see in the lamplight,
    Descending the broad hall stair,
Grave Alice, and laughing Allegra,
    And Edith with golden hair.

A whisper, and then a silence:
  Yet I know by their merry eyes
They are plotting and planning together
  To take me by surprise.

A sudden rush from the stairway,
  A sudden raid from the hall!
By three doors left unguarded
  They enter my castle wall!

They climb up into my turret
  O'er the arms and back of my chair;
If I try to escape, they surround me;
  They seem to be everywhere.

They almost devour me with kisses,
    Their arms about me entwine,
Till I think of the Bishop of Bingen
    In his Mouse-Tower on the Rhine!

Do you think, O blue-eyed banditti,
    Because you have scaled the wall,
Such an old mustache as I am
    Is not a match for you all!

I have you fast in my fortress,
    And will not let you depart,
But put you down into the dungeon
    In the round-tower of my heart.

And there will I keep you forever,
    Yes, forever and a day,
Till the walls shall crumble to ruin,
    And moulder in dust away!

Henry Wadsworth Longfellow

The poet is imagining he is like a castle his daughters have come to raid. The Bishop of Bingen was rumoured to have been kept in a tower and eaten by mice!

My Shadow

I have a little shadow that goes in and out with me,
And what can be the use of him is more than I can see.
He is very, very like me from the heels up to the head;
And I see him jump before me, when I jump into my bed.
The funniest thing about him is the way he likes to grow –
Not at all like proper children, which is always very slow;
For he sometimes shoots up taller like an india-rubber ball,
And he sometimes goes so little that there's none of
    him at all.

He hasn't got a notion of how children
    ought to play,
And can only make a fool of me in every
    sort of way.
He stays so close behind me, he's a coward
    you can see;

I'd think shame to stick to nursie as that shadow sticks to me!
One morning, very early, before the sun was up,
I rose and found the shining dew on every buttercup;
But my lazy little shadow, like an arrant sleepy-head,
Had stayed at home behind me and was fast asleep in bed.

Robert Louis Stevenson

Arrant
complete

A Good Boy

I woke before the morning, I was happy all the day,
I never said an ugly word, but smiled and stuck to play.

And now at last the sun is going down behind the wood,
And I am very happy, for I know that I've been good.

My bed is waiting cool and fresh, with linen smooth and fair,
And I must be off to sleepsin-by, and not forget my prayer.

I know that, till tomorrow I shall see the sun arise,
No ugly dream shall fright my mind, no ugly sight my eyes.

But slumber hold me tightly till I waken in the dawn,
And hear the thrushes singing in the lilacs round the lawn.

Robert Louis Stevenson

Tumbling

In jumping and tumbling
We spend the whole day,
Till night by arriving
Has finished our play.
What then? One and all,
There's no more to be said,
As we tumbled all day,
So we tumble to bed.

Anonymous

Index of First Lines